BEGINNINGS

A Poetry Collection

by Connor Soohoo

First Printing: July 2012

Table of Contents

Introduction

In the beginning, before I wrote poetry for Creative Writing 161, I perceived that poems exclusively expressed serious and abstract concepts or dealt with romantic subjects. My first poems, on the other hand, detailed topics in my everyday life – flowers, toast, the sun, and writer's block. I found that not only did I enjoy writing these whimsical poems, my classmates enjoyed listening to them as well. I believe my most successful works brought everyday objects and situations to life with humor. I discovered a new meaning to poetry. Rather than being an explanation of intangible subjects, I learned that poetry can successfully be an expression of the observations of the world around the writer. Poetry can produce enjoyable emotions that everyone, young or old, man or woman, can experience. Please enjoy the beginnings of my poetry, a collection of my first works.

Haiku

First were tiny buds,

But monsoon rains transformed them

To vibrant blossoms.

Leftover

Oh little piece of toast, you are past your prime.
It has been so long since that fateful lunchtime.
But leaving you to waste would be such a crime.

A Cinquain about Poems (type 1)

Poems,
Simple verses
conveying complex themes,
while still holding truths.
Amazing.

Torn

Under fathoms of soil and mud lies a

Tattered city of lore.

Once a shining standard of the world,

Paragon of society and community,

Is now gone. Destroyed by greed, now

A hollow shell of its former greatness.

Memory of the Sun

Neon rays pierce the tops of blue waves
Giving hope to those dwelling below,
Who dance and frolic around the beams
Worshipping the almighty sunlight.

Offering thanks to those who love him,
The sun god touches the tiny fish,
Turning their scales shiny and golden,
Making them over in his image.

Forevermore the gliding goldfish,
Glistening, dancing, gems of sunshine,
Lighting the murky ocean fathoms,
Memory of the sun in the sea.

The Anti-Poem

Short Couplets are so tough to craft.
Hour after hour, draft after draft.

Too many ideas clog my head,
Writing an anti-one instead.

Dungeons and dragons are too old.
One on nature would be too bold.

I wrote some sci-fi just last week.
Couplets on death are just to bleak.

Technology poem... too dry.
Should I write one about a fly?

I've changed my mind multiple times.
I'm plagued by lack of useful rhymes.

With these words I hope to convey,
All the problems I had today.

Sounds of Life

A medley of simple sounds,
Echo throughout the world
Describing things of all backgrounds.
An entire universe unfurled.

Pitter-patter of light summer rain,
Moan of the evening breeze,
Rumble of bison on the vast prairie plain,
Buzz of the honey bees,

Honking of cars on the crowded freeway,
Blaring of music at intense parties,
Whoosh of a golf ball towards the fairway,
The joy of children devouring brownies,

Clash and clang of metal on metal.
Chatter of guns on the harsh battlefield
Sounds of terror worthy of the devil.
Screams of the wounded left unhealed.

Sweet melody of human laughter
Cry of a life that has just begun
Satisfaction of a life lived happily ever after
And the delighted sigh of a job well done.

Night Class

Twas the hour before night class and all through the hall,
Not a creature was stirring, not even a narwhal.
The chairs were placed in their spots with great care
in hopes that visitors would soon be there.

The students were off preparing their crafts
from food to critiques to poems or drafts,
Hoping and praying for the elusive five stars,
Or making the selection for tonight's food bazaar.

And when the hour struck that fateful six,
Came the trickling flow of the first critics.
Their arrival, slow at first, like a turtle's crawl.
For some were in traffic, others AWOL.

They flocked to this place to listen and hear
readings of their own tales as well as their peers'.
To give and to take some helpful feedback
while munching on a light meager snack.

Setting our chairs into a crescent moon,
We gathered 'round to form our commune,
and waited, silent, with bated breath
to hear glorious tales of adventure and death.

And when all was said and all was done
we bid our goodbyes to the midnight sun,
And headed home for the day, tired but glad
With grins on our faces from the time we just had.

www.ingramcontent.com/pod-product-compliance
Ingram Content Group UK Ltd.
Pitfield, Milton Keynes, MK11 3LW, UK
UKHW040557210726
13854UKWH00007B/1062